MW01231836

The Second Cup
Personal Leadership Brew

Thirty-one Days of
Energy-Enhancing Performance Coaching Messages
Especially Blended for Peak Performance

Mike Malinchok

Certified Professional Executive Coach

Edited by Don Munro
Images by Jennifer S. Beavers

authorHOUSE®

AuthorHouse™
1663 Liberty Drive
Bloomington, IN 47403
www.authorhouse.com
Phone: 1-800-839-8640

Published by AuthorHouse   1/31/2012

ISBN: 978-1-4685-3100-8 (sc)
ISBN: 978-1-4685-3101-5 (e)

Library of Congress Control Number: 2011962910

For S and the two Ks,
the ones who make it matter most

and

With gratitude to the third K
for keeping the embers stoked

INTRODUCTION

Welcome to *The Second Cup*, a collection of daily coaching messages designed to stimulate your thoughts, engage your emotions and serve as a catalyst to help you manifest your best leadership qualities each and every day.

About the name, *The Second Cup*:

I have a passion for coffee.

Everything about it resonates with me … the arresting aroma, the organic connection to the earth, the soothing warmth, the societal camaraderie … everything. Drinking coffee is much more than an act of physical consumption, in my opinion…..it is an act that carries with it our own personal, deeply imbedded rituals that form the foundation of our intellectual, social and emotional connection to the world.

If you're anything like me, while the first cup of coffee in the morning provides the physical boost to get you moving, it's the second cup that finds its way into my brain to engage my thoughts to tackle the day.

And, it's during that second cup of coffee that I tend to

have the most valuable insights…it's when solutions seem to emerge.

So my intention with The Second Cup is to give the reader a similar 'second cup' emotionally energetic boost.

The collection of messages in this book comes from my weekly coaching newsletter, of the same name.

After publishing my first newsletter a few years ago, a good friend sent me a message that included a reference to an ancient Himalayan tradition that speaks to the symbolism attached to the act of sharing cups of tea. According to the tradition, sharing a cup of tea with someone for the first time means that you are strangers.

Sharing a second cup of tea means you are friends.

I consider the time invested in reading my newsletter to be a sign that we have become friends. My commitment to that friendship is to honor the reader's time by presenting material that is timely, relevant and personal – and , delivered in an efficient, compelling, and easily consumed style.

When selecting the messages for this book from the library of newsletter editions, I used three criteria to make my choices:

1. Each message in this book has generated a number of personal responses that represents at least 30% of the subscriber base at the time of publishing, which told me that the specific message is **timely and resonates**.

2. Each message has generated at least one personal response that indicated a significant shift in a personal performance, resulting in tangible benefits, which told me that the content is **relevant and applicable**.

3. Each message has a deep personal connection to me that I felt compelled to share because it brought about some type of a shift in me, which confirms that the content is **personal, not just theoretical**.

The 31 messages are arranged to provide you with the flexibility to either consume the content sequentially or approach each reading based on a topic that supports a situation you may be facing on a given day.

Thank you for sharing your second cup with me….I hope you enjoy!

Mike Malinchok
Certified Professional Executive Coach

Mike Malinchok is President of S2K Performance Coaching, LLC, which focuses on providing support to organizations in the areas of **leadership development, executive coaching, and change management**. He is a graduate of The American University in Washington, DC, and is a Certified Professional Executive Coach. He trained at The Institute for Professional Excellence in Coaching (IPEC). Malinchok's diverse coaching practice includes one-on-one, group, and strategic team coaching for executives seeking peak performance levels in their professional as well as personal lives.

Malinchok has spent over 25 years in the meetings and travel industry in key positions at companies like StarCite, GetThere, BCD Meetings & Incentives, and McGettigan Partners. He has focused most of his career in the area of meetings technology and the business processes surrounding the usage of those technologies. Mike is a frequent speaker at many corporate travel industry events and is considered one of the foremost experts in the area of strategically managed meetings programs (SMMP) for corporations.

He lives in Bucks County, Pennsylvania.

Contents

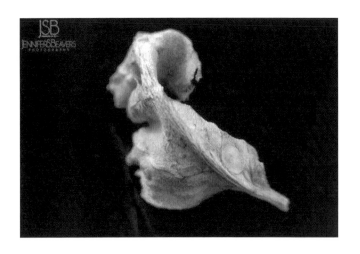

Message 1

EMOTIONS

… like managing a bunch of third-graders

I know an executive whose company has recently undergone an organizational restructure, and I have done some leadership work with him. After five years of working in a position with no direct reports, he now is managing 21 field-based sales professionals. His new responsibilities mean he has to carefully apportion a finite amount of energy on any given day. He is frustrated by the level of emotional energy he has to expend in his multiple daily interactions with his new team. He says: "It's like managing a bunch of third-graders."

To be a truly effective leader, you not only have to be aware of your own emotions, but you also need to be conscious of how the emotions of those you are leading impact their own work performance and interactions.

Awareness of these emotions is the first step in learning to respond—not react—to them.

What my client was coming up against on a daily basis were a series of emotional triggers that all managers should be aware of.

Because most of us aren't readily aware of or easily admit to how these triggers are influencing our behavior, it is easy to interpret how people act out these emotions as immature, narrow-minded, or like a bunch of third-graders.

Let's look at four key emotional triggers or drivers and explore what they might be trying to tell you.

Fear is a means of self-protection, and also a way to find out what you truly value. When you're afraid, look at what you fear losing, and you'll learn about your values, as well as the attachments you have in life.

Anger is born out of love of self or others. When you're angry, it's because you feel that someone or something is a threat to yourself or someone or something that you love or value.

Guilt helps you decide who you are. You feel guilty when you say or do something that goes against who you want to be, or who you think you should be.

Sadness (or grief) helps you remember your vulnerability in this world. They keep things in perspective and give you the opportunity to grow.

As a leader, try this experiment: Over the next few days, be especially conscious of when you are interacting with someone whose behavior or actions may be the result of one or more of the above four emotions.
Then, instead of simply reacting, try responding to what might really be going on. See how that impacts your ability to lead through the situation.

Thanks for sharing your second cup with me.

Message 2

BOOKS THAT FIND YOU

In the fall of 2011, I was experiencing a mixed bag of emotions due to some big changes in my family life. My oldest (son) had gone off to college and my youngest (daughter) joined her older sister as a fellow high school student.

My job description as father underwent a re-write during this time of transition and changes. Suddenly, I had to meet different requirements, deliverables, and timelines based on a new set of life conditions.

Times of transition tend to bring about anxiety, stress, and a lack of clarity that can be very disconcerting.

For me, times of transition are when books come in handy. They provide insight, ideas, validation, and even for a bit of escape.

My experience has been that the most impactful and important books I have read have been the ones that somehow *found me*, not the other way around.

Typically, those books haven't been on *The New York Times* bestseller list. Nor have they been the works of well-known authors. Rather, they've been pretty obscure, and have somehow found their way onto my radar screen.

They are the books that, when I think about it, I can immediately recall where I was when *they* found me, what situation I was facing, and one or two key takeaways that I incorporated into my life.

In preparation for taking my son to college, I reached for two such books on my shelf that found me over 15 years prior – when I was trying to strategize what kind of father I would be to my young children. How ironic!

Once again, these books worked their magic – this time, though, in a fresh way that reconnected me with the broad, deep sense of purpose I have about my role as a father versus the emotional focus in which I was caught up.

They helped to restore clarity.
What powerful, thought-provoking books have found you?
Where were you when they found you?
How did they impact you?

Perhaps today, one or both of the two books that found me were intended to make an appearance on your radar screen:

Letters to My Son: A Father's Wisdom on Manhood, Life, and Love
by Kent Nerburn
-Found me in a bohemian book store in Ketchum, Idaho, and I read it in front of a roaring fire in a ski lodge in Sun Valley.

Strong Fathers, Strong Daughters: 10 Secrets Every Father Should Know by Margaret J. Meeker - Found me in a marketplace book shop on Hawaii's Kona-Kohala coast and read while watching the surf at the Hualālai Resort.

Thanks for sharing your second up with me.

Message 3

SUFFERING

What is the source of all suffering?

According to Buddhist philosophy, it can be as simply put as:
the desire for that which we don't have.

You must have a list, yes? A bigger house; a smaller house; a larger paycheck; less stress; a thinner waist; a fatter checkbook; to be older; to be younger; to be wiser; to be more popular; to be more disciplined; to be able to relax more; to have more time for self; to have more people in your life; to be in a relationship; to have peace of mind;

to be respected; to be validated; or to be heard, seen or understood.

Digging at this a little deeper, it is fairly clear to see how some
might go to a place that says: All of life is suffering.

Now, think about this principle:

In life, pain is inevitable, suffering is optional.
*(Wow! That just might make Siddhārtha Gautama[1] unfold
from his meditation posture and reach for a bag of Doritos!)*

How we view the suffering in our life is a foundational philosophy upon which we manifest our leadership style.

Think about the way in which you lead (as a parent, as a manager, or as a CEO): Ask yourself these questions:

- What am I suffering from or what am I desiring that I don't have which places me in this leadership role?

(Dig deep, and understand the WHY of your leadership.)

- What role do the people I lead play in the attainment of my own desires, or the relieving of my suffering?

Now, take a step outside of yourself:

Try to understand the suffering or desires of the people you lead? (career growth, attainment of money

1   Spiritual teacher from ancient India who founded Buddhism.

or recognition or respect, etc.), and see how their
accomplishment of what you need them to do affects their
own desires.

This is powerful! It is **important,** and it will open you up
to a potentially new way of looking at how you lead.

Lead your folks toward the desired goal in a way that
validates, honors, and supports how it is tied directly into
their own
personal desires/goals – not just your own.

Think about the enormously powerful position you are in
as a leader – not only to engage others to help you alleviate
your own suffering, but also to help them alleviate their
own suffering in the process.

It's an awesome position.
Understand it, absorb it into your psyche, and then
allow it to manifest through your leadership style.

Thanks for sharing your second cup with me.

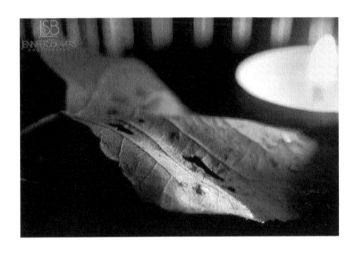

Message 4

LOVE

*the **fuel** of leadership*

Let's take a look at a few ways love can be defined:
- To have an intense emotional attachment to someone or something
- To like or desire enthusiastically
- To thrive on
- A strong positive emotion of regard and affection
- To get pleasure from someone or something

How would you answer this question:

Why do you do what you do for a living?
Some answers could be:
- I love the money
- I love the security
- I'm good at it and feel successful
- It's better than (fill in the blank)
- I enjoy the prestige
- I love the routine and predictability.

The answer reveals something for which you have an attachment to, a desire for, or derive pleasure from. There is something that you *love* that has manifested through what you do.

Now, go deeper into this and identify what that love makes possible for you by completing a sentence such as those below:

I love the money, because it allows me to_____.
I love the security, which enables me to_____.
When I feel successful, I can_____.

The way you complete the sentences will give you good insight into the true love you have and how it is fueling what you do and how you do it.

As a leader of your own life, your family, your team, or your company, it is this type of self-awareness that will inspire others to achieve their potential. It will lead others to their own greatness, and, like nothing else, enable your true, loving character to impact the world with powerful ripples.

Today , I encourage you to lead with love in <u>every</u> relationship in your life – with your own self, your children, your significant other, your team, your competitors, your co-workers and, perhaps most powerfully of all, with someone whose pain you are in a position to ease.

Thanks for sharing your second cup with me.

Message 5

TRUST

Self-trust is the first secret of success.
- Ralph Waldo Emerson

I suggest that Emerson's quote could be expanded to include two additional trust place holders that are worth examining: trust in others and trust in the universe (or any higher power).

First, a definition of trust:

Reliance on the integrity, strength, ability, surety, etc., of a person or thing; confidence.

I'd like to suggest that you think about the questions below to help you become aware of how your leadership style may be impacted by your level of trust in yourself, in those around you who share your journey and in the broader concept of the universe.

Your answers to the questions that follow are designed to trigger insight and awareness. There are no right or wrong answers.

SELF: How well do you trust yourself as a leader?
- To what extent do you understand your role and how it connects to the broader goals of your organization?
- How well are you able to articulate your vision? How can you tell when your vision is understood and shared?
- How do you know that your expectations and timelines are understood and agreed to?

OTHERS: How much do you trust your team?
- What do you know unequivocally about each person you lead, for example, their integrity, motivation, and work ethic.
- What are the top two tangible traits of each team member?
- How well does the team assignments match up with top traits identified above?

THE UNIVERSE: In what way does the universe conspire to impact your success?
- How does your belief system in a higher power or a greater universe drive your thoughts?
- In general, do you come from a place of abundance, or scarcity? Is the glass half full or half empty?
- When one door closes, do you envision anything

opening as compensation, for example, another door, a window, a peep hole?

Your ability to trust will have a direct impact on how effectively you can lead versus staying mired down in the minutia of your workplace.

Today, check your trust levels. Try to see where there may be some deficiencies that are limiting your effectiveness.

Thanks for sharing your second cup with me.

Message 6

BEING SEEN

"There you are" … or … "Here I am."

A very good friend shared with me the perspective that there are two types of people in the world:

One kind walks into a cocktail party and proclaims "**Here I am!**" and the other kind walks into that same cocktail party and says: **"There you are!"**

One could be considered to be compelling, charismatic, and dynamic, while the other could be said to be inspiring, engaging, and memorable.
(Notice how all six adjectives could be applied to both types.)

Basically, the same types of leaders exist. We have all most likely encountered the first type of leader in our careers. It is the most common leadership style in many organizations.

I'm finding that far too few people have had the experience of being led and influenced by the second type.

Truly impactful leaders are the ones who **connect with people one-on-one**.

The great ones are those who can turn a single conversation into the catalyst for launching an entire organizational shift in thinking.

A few external traits I've noticed that are relatively easy to spot in a

There you are! leader:
- **Active engagement** at all levels of the organization
- **Personal involvement** with team members in order to deliver results
- **Genuine interest** in the well-being of each contributing member of the team
- **Unbroken connection** to the team's mindset for achieving the established goals

- You need to look in the most intimate place – your own heart and mind – to identify when you're in the presence of a *There you are!* leader.

It's the truly great leaders that ignite a powerful sensation within you … that inspire your thoughts, fuel your emotions, and ultimately drive your actions.

.

There you are! leaders instill thoughts that are inspiring,

uplifting, and positive. Those feelings drive a desire in you to somehow do better, be more, or work harder to get the kind of outcomes that are
manifestations of your deepest desires.

You'll know you're in the presence of a *There you are* leader when you find yourself remembering the **greatness within you. It's** like he or she has walked into a cocktail party and was able to spot you out of a crowded room and say …
"There you are!"
Thanks for sharing your second cup with me.

Message 7

CONTRADICTION

Creating space for duality … it's always both.

How comfortable are you with contradictions? Are you someone who seeks out the definitive answers that leave little room for interpretation or complexity? Or are you the kind of person that is able to roam freely in the gray areas of life and business?

One of the most stifling words in the English language is the word *but.*.Take a look at the restrictive nature of how this small word negates, diminishes, and dismisses the powerful words preceeding it. As you read each sentence pay close attention to how the word BUT impacts your feelings about what you've just read:

*We have hit our sales quota for the year, **BUT**, our T&E spend is 25% over budget.*

.

*Mary is an excellent public speaker, **BUT** she embellishes facts.*

*We finally landed that new target account, **BUT** it's going to be a resource drain on the account team.*

*I have lost 15 pounds, **BUT** I have 15 more to lose.*

Notice that the second half of each sentence implants the subtle suggestion that the first half of the content might somehow be suspect or somewhat less because of what follows the BUT. How might this influence your response to the news in the first half of the sentence?
As a leader, it's important to recognize that there **will always be contradictions**, conflicting impacts, and opportunity costs for our successes.

There is rarely a situation that is pure black or pure white … all good or all bad … totally positive or totally negative. And the people we lead will be **robust fusions** of many qualities and character traits that both impress us and challenge our patience.
I suggest that you consider recognizing **the power of contradictions** as a way of leading your team toward a more open, dynamic, and collaborative way of working.

It is subtle, yet dramatic, to accept situations as being black AND white, good AND bad, positive AND negative.
Take a look at how simply replacing the word **BUT** with the word '**AND**' changes the entire tone of the earlier

sentences. Just as before, pay attention to your feelings toward what you read below:

*We have hit our sales quota for the year, **AND** the T&E spend is 25% over budget.*

*Mary is an excellent public speaker, **AND** she embellishes facts.*
*We finally landed that new target account, **AND** it's going to be a resource drain on the account team.*
*I have lost 15 pounds, **AND** I have 15 more to lose.*

The small, but inclusive word **AND** creates the space and gives permission to embrace both parts of each sentence, without diminishing or negating the value and role of either.

Thanks for sharing your second cup with me.

Message 8

IS ANYONE LISTENING?

Some of the Time

During times of change and strife, strong leadership comes from those who not only **have a message** but can **stay on message**.

Sometimes that is easier said than done. Market conditions, team dynamics, organizational pressures, and family demands can all conspire to **derail the very voice that most needs to be heard**.

Have you ever questioned **whether you are being heard**? Do you wonder if your messages are **having the desired impact**? Are there times when you doubt whether **those you lead are listening**?
We often look for evidence of how our messages are

impacting those we lead. And sometimes that evidence can be elusive … but it's important to know that it **is** there.

Consider these 10 perspectives on leadership messages:

#1 Sometimes the impact of the message is not mine to know.

#2 Sometimes the message that most powerfully resonates with me is met with indifference.

#3 Sometimes my message deeply impacts those whom I didn't even know were listening.

#4 Sometimes there's an inverse relationship between the amount of time put into crafting the message and the depth of its impact.

#5 Sometimes silence is the most powerful message.

#6 Sometimes timing is magic.

#7 Sometimes the most vocal critics of the message are the most loyal supporters of the messenger.

#8 Sometimes it's hard not to take it personally when people seem indifferent to your message.

#9 Sometimes receiving feedback (of any kind) is more energizing than a second cup of strong coffee.

#10 Sometimes I must accept the truth that I cannot control the impact of my messages.

What is clear to me is that there are just three things about messages that we have any level of control over:

- The **<u>intention</u>** behind them
- The **<u>clarity</u>** with which they are articulated
- The **<u>consistency of purpose</u>** for which they are delivered

- Thanks for sharing your second cup with me.

Message 9

ACCESS

Are you there?

Main office line, private office line, business cell phone, home land line, personal cell phone, business email, private email #1, private email #2, call waiting, text messaging, Facebook, LinkedIn, i-Meet …

Exactly how many access paths do you have open for communication to you? Take a moment and count them up.

Now, take an honest assessment of how frequently you check one or more of those paths in the course of a typical hour. .

We can't escape the fact that as we grow in our careers and gain leadership responsibilities, we open up more and more paths of access....and, our culture has accepted that 24x7x365 access has become the base level of expectation.

Sometimes, though, instant access can bring with it the potential for instant inaccuracy. In our zeal to demonstrate instant accessibility, we often forgo taking the time and perspective to craft a response, and so we compromise accuracy.

A simple question: which is more important: Access or accuracy?

For most executives today, the answer is both....they are expected to be both accessible and accurate 100% of the time. Try as we may, though, this type of expectation can rarely be met consistently for the long haul.
Early in my career, I had the luxury of having a well-trained elegantly mannered secretary who would screen or hold all my calls if there was an urgent business task that required my full attention. Her job was to manage ACCESS to me so that I could focus my energy on accuracy in my job.

Having someone else to manage our access is a luxury long gone for most of us, and we all must determine at what point we will 'hold all calls', 'shut our doors', and turn off all access in order to focus on accuracy .

Which of the following statements about your accessibility most closely aligns with who you are as a leader in your organization or to your clients or family?

1) You are always accessible whether or not you are in a position to provide accurate information.
2) You have limited accessibility and are known for delivering highly accurate information on your own time table.
3) Your accessibility is limited and varies based on whatever is holding your attention at the moment.
4) Your accessibility is structured and monitored as a means of managing accuracy of information

The next time you reach for your device to check your email or text messages, take a moment to think whether your access or your accuracy is what is most important **at that very moment.**

Think about it the next time you feel that buzz in your pocket or purse.
Thanks for sharing your second cup.

Message 10

GOALS

New Year's Resolutions Don't Work!

The idea of using January 1 as a time to establish goals and resolutions for ourselves has evolved into a cultural and financial phenomenon. Fitness clubs, smoking cessation product manufacturers, and weight loss organizations all show record sales figures in January as the energy put into self improvement resolutions is at its peak for the year.

As most of us know all too well........by February the fitness clubs are back to normal usage levels, cigarette consumption is back up, and older inefficient life habits are showing up again.

It's easy to chalk this up to human nature and make self-effacing jokes that allow us to refrain from doing the challenging self-work that will allow us to make truly lasting changes.

Today, I'd like you to look at just one resolution you made and answer the some questions. They might open up some insight to help you get to the root of the change that's needed in order to accomplish your goals.

Try it with one … then, go on to every resolution you've made.

Question #1: How will the attainment of this goal (resolution) enhance your career and/or your life? Be as specific as possible using all five senses in your description of your life upon attainment of this goal.

Question #2: In what ways will the key relationships in your life (family, boss, friends) be impacted by your attainment of this goal (resolution)? Think about whether any relationships will change, grow, or end … and whether its attainment opens up the possibility of new relationships entering your life.

Question #3: What is preventing you from having the life and relationships you described in questions 1 & 2 – Right now? What impact does your stated goal (resolution) have on the roadblocks that are in your way?

Question #4: What is the pain associated with taking the kinds of actions necessary to reach your goal?

What changes do you need to make in order to hit your goal? What must you give up in order to 'get' your goal?

<u>Question #5: What is the pain associated with not taking any action toward your goal and keeping things status quo?</u> What is it that led you to make this resolution in the first place?

New Year's resolutions don't work … unless, you're willing enough to do the work, as revealed in the questions above.

Thanks for sharing your second cup with me.

Message 11

PERSONAL BRAND

Regardless of age, position, or the business we happen
to be in, all of us need to understand the importance of
branding. We are CEO's of
our own companies:
Me Inc.
As author Tom Peters says, "To be in business today, our
most important job is to be head marketer for the brand
called _you_."

In today's virtual world, the manner in which both
business and personal relationships are defined and
cultivated has moved away from the traditional face-to-
face interactive methods to the new mediums that focus
more on sound bites of information.
**Online profiles have become the billboards of who we
are** and have laid the foundation for what has become
known as the personal brand.

While the term may be a new one, the concept behind
it is not. Effective leaders have always been aware of and
paid attention to the key factors that go into the makings

of a personal brand and did so without the use of the slick moniker.

At the most basic level, your personal brand is the unspoken commitment that you make to anyone you come in contact with ... it is your promise of quality, consistency, competency, and reliability. In previous generations, it was simply referred to as 'reputation'. But, in today's information-based environment, reputation is just one component of an individual's personal brand.

I encourage you to review the following six components that make up PERSONAL BRANDING and reflect on the questions to help you gain clarity around your own.

#1 Packaging - In what ways does your outward appearance reflect the image and level of quality that you want to convey? Without knowing you personally, what would someone presume about you based on how you present yourself (both in person and in an online profile)?

#2 Credentials - Including education, work experience, accreditations, and professional certifications, how do your credentials support the level of credibility and expertise you want to have associated with your personal brand?

#3 Reputation - What attributes are you consistently known for? Name three *absolutes that* anyone who knows you, has worked with you, or is familiar with you would say about your work or priorities.

#4 Spokespeople - Who talks about you and what do they say? By what method do you pick who you use as a professional and personal reference or spokesperson?

#5 Alliances/Partnerships - Examine each professional and personal alliance (e.g. partnerships, colleagues, friends). Why do you choose to engage in those relationships? In what way does each affiliation reinforce your personal brand?

#6 Avocations/Altruisms - In what ways do you invest your free time, and why? What might someone infer from knowing your hobbies, charitable or volunteer interests, or recreational activities?

If you had to describe your own brand in terms of a retail product, what would it be? And, what would your packaging look like? Why?
What buzz words would adorn the label, and at what type of store would your product be available? What would your price point be? And, lastly, what would your warranty look like?
This is a worthy exercise because the questions will help you think of a comparison to a familiar product you like. Often, the products or services we gravitate toward provide clues into our own personal brand or value proposition.

Thanks for sharing your second cup with me.

Message 12

CHARISMA

Charisma comes from effective leadership; it's not the other way around.

I attended a conference where I had the opportunity to observe and listen to a variety of professionals speak who are in leadership positions. While their leadership skills were of varied levels and their specific talents pretty diverse, as I sat through the sessions, I found myself thinking:

What **makes me want to keep listening to what this person has to say**?

Further, I asked myself, To what extent is their personal
charisma engaging me or
causing my attention to lapse?

Looking at a few definitions of charisma sheds light on
how important it is for any leader to understand his or her
own unique, personal type of charisma that is impacting
their leadership effectiveness:

Definition 1:
A rare personal quality attributed to leaders who arouse
fervent popular devotion and enthusiasm.

Definition 2:
A trait found in people whose personalities are
characterized by a personal charm and magnetism, along
with innate and powerfully sophisticated abilities of
interpersonal communication and persuasion.

Definition 3:
Originally a term from Christian theology, meaning
a favour specially given by God's grace, the word was
appropriated to mean 'a certain quality of an individual
personality by virtue of which he is set apart from
ordinary men and treated as endowed with supernatural ...
or ... exceptional powers or qualities.

These definitions aroused in me a strong sense of
caution. Words like rare, fervent, magnetism, persuasion,
supernatural, and set apart suggest that charisma is
something dramatic, kind of theatrical in nature, and can
sometimes be used to manipulate people.

Yet, the speakers who engaged me the most at the

conference did NOT display characteristics that would have been described using any of the above words.

Not too long ago, I asked my teenage daughter to name the teachers she's had that she considers most charismatic. After she listed several names, I asked her to rank them, and her answer was brilliant in its clarity and simplicity:

She said: "Dad, they're all charismatic in their own way."

Try this definition on:

One who is charismatic is said to be capable of using their personal being, rather than just speech or logic alone, to interface with other human beings in a personal and direct manner, and effectively communicate a position and vision to them.

So, here's a question I encourage you to think about and answer:

In what ways, does my own charisma manifest in my professional and personal life?

Thanks for sharing your second cup with me.

Message 13

SALESMANSHIP

A long personal saga came to a close one rainy Saturday afternoon when I wrote out a check to purchase a new sofa.

To some, this may sound like a non-event, but I am someone who finds purchasing furniture to be among life's most intimidating tasks. Every insecurity that lurks in my subconscious surfaces when faced with taking on the furniture sales guy or hitting the purchase button online.

But that all came to a halt when I met Helen at the local furniture store.

Helen was a comfortable amalgamation of my mother, my favorite aunt, and my third grade teacher.

Within seconds I could feel that I was in the hands of a true sales professional who was going to lead me through this interaction ... and I was able to relax.

In 43 minutes, Helen brought to an end my seven weeks of frustration and confusion. As I walked out of the store with my receipt and delivery confirmation sheet in hand, I was very much aware of how well Helen led me through this process.

Throughout the rest of the day, I thought about the way in which she managed our exchange. I was able to break it down into the following key things she did that resulted not only with the sale, but in creating one of those moment-of-truth type of

experiences that create customers for life.

1. She approached me **respectfully and carefully.**
Her open-ended questions made me feel as though she was interested in learning about what problem a sofa purchase would solve for me. There was no false niceties or meaningless chatter to fill the silence.

2. She made it **personal.**
Because she listened carefully to what I both said and didn't say, she picked up on all of the information I shared to shift the conversation completely into my world, less about a sofa, and more about my family, my home, and me.

3. She **paid attention** to me.
She successfully read my body language and reactions to each sofa she showed me until I told her I'd found the one I wanted.

4. She **validated what she heard** from me.
Before closing the deal, she suggested I snap a picture with my phone and send it to my key stakeholders – my two daughters, who head up the home décor committee, and who were vital to my decision.

5. She **stayed with me** after the sale.
The deal was closed, but she continued to honor me after the

*sale with respect, consideration, and time by walking me to
my car and telling me why my choice was a good one.*

Helen is a true <u>leader</u> in her profession -
a sales <u>professional</u> in every sense of the word.

Thanks for sharing your second cup with me.

Message 14

PRIORITIES

I almost missed a life-affirming weekend with family because I think I'm so busy and so important and have so much on my plate.)

I returned from a weekend trip that I should not have taken. It was two days that had put me behind the proverbial 8-ball with client deliverables, presentation preparation, and the never-ending pile of laundry. By all practical accounts, I should have been at my desk spending the two days writing a proposal, crafting an upcoming speech, and getting things done around the house.

Instead, I spent the weekend in New York celebrating my
niece's birthday and recent engagement.

**I almost missed a life-affirming weekend with family
because I think I am so busy and so important and
have so much on my plate.**
The catalyst for my decision to ditch the work and go to
the family celebration was a YouTube video link that a
friend had sent to me. It was a seven minute recording
of a surprise event at a wedding in which the groom, the
groom's father, and the bride's father surprised the bride
and her mother by staging the singing of "Sunrise, Sunset"
from the play *Fiddler on the Roof.*
What starts out as a quiet, poignant serenade by the
men to their wives progresses quickly into an elaborate
theatrical production involving the entire bridal party –
complete with choreography, lighting, and costumes.

I really wanted to think that these people couldn't possibly
be as busy or important as me and, therefore, had the time
to devote to the planning and
execution of the production.

But the practical side of me noticed the lavish setting and
well-heeled participants and it was clear to me this was a
successful, professional crowd who probably had a life load
that was similar to my own.

So, by what force of nature was this group
led to create such a life-affirming event?

I believe it was the leadership team of
the groom, his father, and father-in-law. In one sense, you
could say they were their own organization.

These guys not only managed to fulfill the textbook roles that the wedding planner laid out for them, they also reached very deep inside of themselves to create a life-affirming moment for their family, their guests, and (thanks to YouTube) the world.
They went beyond the norm, exceeded even the highest expectations, not only went outside the box, but crushed that box on their way out.

They demonstrated what, in my opinion, is the most powerful form of leadership: Life-Affirming Leadership.

They brought out the very best in everyone who participated or watched. They touched their hearts, minds, and souls. And, mine, too.

That's powerful leadership.
I am grateful to a very good friend who enabled me to see that I probably wasn't so busy, important, or carrying such a full plate that I couldn't make time for a life-affirming weekend with family. And at least I didn't have to sing or dance.
Thanks for sharing your second cup with me.

Message 15

SELF MADE

On a recent cross-country flight, I read Malcolm Gladwell's book *Outliers: The Story of Success*. My interpretation of the main message is that there's really no such thing as self-made success.
Gladwell states:

"People don't rise from nothing. ... It is only by asking where they are from that we can unravel the logic behind who succeeds and who doesn't."

He provides the analogy of the tallest oak tree in the forest. Yes, there's the organic fact that the tree grew from a pretty hardy acorn. But, that alone wasn't enough to assure its place as the tallest oak tree in the forest. Some other factors that need to be acknowledged are: no other trees blocked its sunlight, the soil around it was deep and rich, no animals chewed through its bark as a sapling, and there were no lumberjacks working in that particular forest during its lifetime.

One of the most powerful leadership exercises I have done and encourage my clients to do is what is called the **gratitude deposit** exercise.
It's simple ... can take very little time ... and yields an astounding
<u>return on your investment (ROI)</u>.

Take a few moments to think about yourself as the acorn referenced above
(smart, ambitious, loving, and talented).

Think about the soil in which you were planted
(your family, your hometown, your neighborhood).

Spend some time identifying the influences around you that nurtured and encouraged your development.

Identify some influences that perhaps simply stayed out of your way
- didn't block your sunlight.

Try to recall those who chewed on your bark, so to speak, and served to toughen you up in ways that have served you well in your life and career.

Now, identify two people who played key roles in enabling you to become
your version of the tallest oak tree.
(Is it your mom, dad? How about your spouse or partner?
A friend? A teacher? A boss? A former stranger?)

Try to put into a succinct statement specifically what they did for you and how it directly impacted your life's path.

Did it inspire, empower, recognize, comfort, encourage,
push, teach, guide, love ... etc.

Now, make a gratitude deposit:
Tell them
in person, by phone or through written word how much it
meant to you.

Keep it simple or else you'll likely get distracted and it
won't happen!

Ken Sychtwald, in his book, <u>*With Purpose*</u>, says the key to
lasting happiness requires you to
"find your core strengths and figure out how to deploy
them."

Let those two people know that they helped you do just
that.

Thanks for sharing your second cup with me.

Message 16

IDENTITY

IN A WORD

Marshall Goldsmith, in his book *Mojo*, refers to reputation as "people's recognition – or rejection – of your identity and achievement."

He further goes on to say that reputations are formed by "a sequence of actions that resemble one another. When other people see a pattern of resemblance, that's when they start forming your reputation."

Notice that he says *they* form your reputation. We don't form our own reputation, although we can influence it greatly.

There's a little party game that I like to play with family

and friends. I call it "In a Word," and it involves going
around the room asking each person to
sum up the guest of honor in a single word.
Simple game = powerfully insightful tool.

What can start out as a light-hearted semantic exercise can
often times reveal just
how diverse a reputation that a single person might have,
and, in some cases, how unaware we might be of the
impact we have on others.

If you have a birthday coming up and you'll be
surrounded by people whose perspective you value,
consider opening yourself up to this insightful game.

Stick to the rule that the description must only consist
of one word; don't allow deviations from that. And have
someone write down all the words so you can reflect back
on them when you have a quiet moment.

Take note of the <u>consistencies and the inconsistencies</u>. Try
to see how and why some folks made the word choices
that they did.

One of the revelations from this exercise is that we don't
always show up the same way to everyone we interact
with.

We have created life compartments within which
we influence our reputation in different ways.

The value of this exercise is in its ability to create
awareness of

the way in which your reputation may be influencing your ability to drive success.

Recognize that your sphere of influence and depth of personal impact just might be different than you assume.

It's worth playing a little game like this.

Thanks for sharing your second cup with me.

Message 17

MILESTONES

Milestones vs. Goals:

A goal defines your purpose and
milestones measure your progress toward that purpose.
**Milestones can be one of the most powerful tools in
driving achievement of goals.** Too often, though, in
our busy work and life situations, we make one of two
mistakes as it relates to milestones.

Either we dismiss milestones as *inconsequential* and
without purpose … or we spend way too much time
celebrating the milestones and
lose sight of the ultimate goal.

Definition:
A milestone (from the Latin *milliarium*) is one of a series

of numbered markers placed along a road or boundary at intervals of one mile. Milestones are constructed to provide **reference points** along the road that can be used to reassure travelers that **the proper path is being followed** or, conversely, **a mid-course adjustment is required**.

Thinking in terms of milestones can help you organize your activities and available resources into **a logical sequence of steps or stages**.

It can also serve as **a powerful motivator** to move you or your team away from destructive inertia when goals seem out of reach.

Recently I hit a personal milestone when I ran a 5K race for autism awareness at a local park.

A busy work schedule with demanding travel requirements has jeopardized my ability to hit a personal health goal that I've set for myself this year. Those health goals were big-picture, strategic and caused me much stress as I got further away from attainment.

Problem was: I had no in-between step from my current state to the goal I had set. So, I **lost focus and began the process of rationalizing the impending failure,** and I began embracing my age as a viable justification.

That's where a milestone helped. A far less daunting distance than the marathon I had done a few years ago, the 5K race got me to lace up my sneakers and walk out the door (Some say that is the hardest part of any workout.).

It gave me a **much needed and immediate boost** to move

the dial just a single notch up. And now it's on to the next milestone.

Three key values to milestones to keep in mind:

- Milestones are ***significant*** because they show movement from point A to point B.

- Milestones are ***introspective*** because they give you pause to evaluate your strategy and make necessary adjustments.

- Milestones are ***motivating*** because they are attainable when the bigger goal seems out of reach.

So, try applying some milestone-based thinking to one of your most challenging goals.

Thanks for sharing your second cup with me.

Message 18

FAKING IT

I was attending a leadership development seminar recently where the subject of effective communication skills was on the agenda. During one part of the program, the merits of the
"fake it till you make it" philosophy were debated.

As you probably know, "fake it till you make it" (also sometimes called "act as if") is a common catch phrase that means to imitate confidence so that as the "fake" confidence produces success, it will generate real confidence.
A few years ago, I learned of an interesting experiment conducted by Columbia University in which forty-two male and female participants were randomly assigned to a high- or low-power pose group.

The premise under study in this experiment was the impact of physical posture (or poses) on business performance.

Subjects in the high-power pose group were manipulated

into two expansive poses for one minute each. First, the classic feet on desk, hands behind head. Then -- standing and leaning on one's hands over a desk. Those in the low-power pose group were posed for the time period in two restrictive poses: sitting in a chair with arms held close and hands folded, and standing with arms and legs crossed tightly.

Researchers discovered that holding one's body in expansive, "high-power" poses for as little as two minutes stimulates higher levels of testosterone and lower levels of cortisol. In addition to causing hormonal shifts, power poses lead to increased feelings of power and a greater tolerance for risk.

While this study seems to lend credence to the beliefs that if you act confident, you'll BE confident and "fake it till you make it," I believe it would be lazy leadership to stop there.

Effective leadership is as much about content as it is about style and CONTEXT (or content)?.

Personally, I am much more inclined to embrace a leader's style when their content and credibility are compelling over a polished presenter whose content and credibility don't garner my respect or attention.

I stumbled upon a quote that I believe should be the qualifier to anyone subscribing to the "fake it till you make it" philosophy:

*The best way to sound like you know what you're talking about is
to actually know what you're talking about.*
~Author unknown

Thanks for sharing your second cup with me.

Message 19

SPEAKING WITH PURPOSE

I believe strongly that in every situation where you are asked to deliver a speech, you are in a powerful position to connect with, engage, and influence your audience in a way that makes you an **agent of change**.

And that is something that should never be treated lightly.

You most likely have heard it said many feel that, next to death, public speaking is considered to be **the most stressful thing in life**.

Studies have shown that the most prevalent fears about public speaking center around the risks that you might somehow appear either **foolish** (stumble on words, show vulnerability) or **unqualified** (misstate facts, reveal some gap in knowledge).

Most books, training seminars and courses I've seen on the topic of public speaking tend to focus on one of two areas: 1) the physical movements, postures, and body management of speech making or 2) the organization, layout, and vocabulary used in crafting the content of the speech.

I think there's more to it...

A profoundly impactful speaker is one who has an unshakable, readily evident, and magnetic **sense of purpose** in imparting his or her message.

Before crafting the building blocks of the speech you are to deliver, consider these questions:

What unique perspective do I bring to the topic?

How is it that I came to be selected for this assignment?

What do I know about this topic that cannot be refuted by anyone?

In what way does this topic, situation, or audience connect to my true passion(s) in my life or career?

What can I bring to this speech that no one else in the world can?

At minimum, what do I want my audience to feel the very moment I stop speaking?

The insight from understanding the answers to the above questions will provide the answers to the question that everyone in the audience will be thinking:

Why should I listen to you?

As a speaker, if you fail to answer that question in the first few moments of speaking … you are in an uphill battle to establish yourself as a thought leader, move your audience and become a change agent.

If you're up there speaking with an undeniable sense of purpose, then your experience becomes less about any potential stumbles or missteps and more about the **core message** you're imparting.

Thanks for sharing your second cup with me.

Message 20

QUESTIONS

In my mid-life quest for physical peak performance, I have come to finally accept just recently that nutrition plays as important a role as
physical activity in driving results.

I've learned that GOOD FATS play a vital role in transporting key nutrients through the body to support good health. BAD FATS, conversely, are laden with things that work against the achievement of good health.
So paying attention to the type of fat I consume is a critical component of
good nutrition and peak performance.
As an executive coach, my clients come to me seeking assistance in reaching peak performance – sometimes in their professional lives, and other times in their personal lives.

In order to help them achieve their goals, one of the most important tools I use are questions … the kind that are open-ended, probing, challenging, future-directed, and solution-oriented.

You can look at questions as the equivalent of dietary fats. The good fats bring nutrition, and questions transport information from the source to the seeker in order to gain understanding and insight.

Since information will impact how well I can help my clients achieve their goals, I've come to recognize that good questions like good fats, are *unsaturated* – no bias, no agendas, no confusion, and no lack of clarity.

On the other hand, bad questions are like bad fats. They're both saturated – with not-so-hidden agendas, with self-validating intentions and with judgments.

Good questions are borne out of anabolic energy and reflect big-picture engagement, universal acceptance of what is, and confidence in the ability to benefit from all answers.

Below are six key qualities of good questions for you to review and begin to incorporate into your leadership approach:

1. They cannot be answered in one word, for example, yes or no;

2. They are neutral, having no expected or so-called acceptable answer; they honestly seek information;

3. They are unambiguous, not crafted to trick or confuse or require interpretation;

4. They reflect active listening and understanding;

5. They come from a place of honesty, integrity and respect;

6. They are stand-alone, equally valid both in and out of context;.

Look at the example below and see how each might generate different types of responses:

Good question:
If you land that new client what would that allow for you that's not possible today?
Bad question:
I guess you really want that new client, don't you?

Keep an ear out for bad questions today. Then flip them to good questions and see the difference in how the information (nutrition) flows.
Thanks for sharing your second cup with me.

Message 21

MOTIVATION

*People often say that motivation doesn't last. Well, neither
does bathing - that's why we recommend it daily.*
-- Zig Ziglar

An important part of working with clients as an executive
coach is to help them understand and get comfortable
with the concept of self-coaching.

It is the personal tool kit we each have at our disposal to
keep us motivated, keep our thinking level-headed, and
even give us the "**kick in the butt**" that we sometimes
need.

Below are some of my favorite self-coaching truisms that I
hope will strike a nerve, trigger an action, or remind you
of an
inner resolve that's a little trapped under distractions
right about now:

.

* * * * *

An ineffective, unhappy life is learned - you weren't born that way!

The person you are at this moment is really the end result of all the life choices you've made to date.

Understanding how control and habit can echo through your life is the way toward dismantling the most stubborn, resistant problems.

Another word for boredom is detachment … and boredom is often times an attempt to insulate you from feelings of failure or frustration.

If your healthy instincts are sacrificed to a life of control, sooner or later you will suffer.

Life experience + self-trust = success …
Life experience + self-doubt = struggle.

You become what you think.

Let life unfold … there are <u>obstacles</u>, but no dead ends.

Every problem has a solution, and sometimes I have to wait for an answer.

The greatest strategy for personal and professional development is bold self expression.

Argue your limitations, and they will be yours.

And from the plaque that hangs over the back doorway of my home:

"Be nice or go away."

Thanks for sharing your second cup with me.

Message 22

PARTNERSHIP

It is my experience that the term *strategic partnership* is being used to describe a pretty wide range of business relationships that may or may not fall into the category that I would consider to be true partnerships.
Many business executives when making a pitch take a casual approach to peppering the dialogue with the plethora of strategic partnerships they have in place as a stamp of credibility.

It's as if strategic partnerships has become the business equivalent
to Facebook friends.
Michael Eisner, in his book *Working Together*, presents a compelling blueprint for building strategic partnerships that matter, that last, and that allow each partner to do their very best work.

His book highlights several well known successful strategic partnerships, and what becomes quickly evident is that, while the industries, business situations, and hurdles were unique to each partnership, there are some common threads that ring true to any business today looking at establishing true strategic partnerships. They are:

1. Both parties agree on the definition of partnership, and they commit resources to support that definition.
2. Each partner has a clear understanding of the others' goals and objectives in entering into the partnership. There is clarity of purpose and understanding of anticipated outcomes.
3. The tactical "gives" and "gets" are clear, articulated, and the impact of non-performance on the success of the partnership is understood by all .
4. More than the partnership documentation, the personal relationship between the partners is paramount. It usurps all other business issues. The partners know and care about the state of the relationship at all times.
5. There's an exit strategy; it's clear to both parties what would need to happen in order to bring about an ending to the partnership.

In the end, you could ask: Do strategic partnerships cause the success or does the success sustain the strategic partnership?

In reality, the answer is a little bit of both.

Take an honest look at the business alliances you have in place today. Take an inventory based on the five points above. And then reach out to each partner and have a talk. It's time!

Thanks for sharing your second cup with me.

Message 23

PERSONAL IMPACT

Definition: To have an effect on, alter, or influence.
When my son was in the final stages of selecting a college
to attend, one of his tasks was to conduct personal
interviews with the deans of each
of the top schools he chose.

As we discussed his approach and intentions for the
meetings, we worked together to develop a list of key
questions for him to ask. They would give him the most
relevant information to help him finalize his decision.

On the day that he pulled out of the driveway to head to
the first college interview, I had a flashback to his first day
of kindergarten when (unbeknownst to him) I covertly
followed his bus and discreetly watched from behind a
bush as he arrived at the school and safely got inside the
building.
In more than a few ways, the 12 years in between passed
at what seemed like warp speed. And, it caused me to
pause and reflect on the concept of *personal impact*. In this
case, I spent some time that day thinking about the way

in which my leadership, my teaching, my example, my mistakes, and my inconsistencies have personally impacted the way in which my son is approaching his life.

Whether you are a parent, a manager, a lawyer, a sales associate, a CEO, or a barista (an expert coffee maker and server), it is vital to your success to be conscious of the way in which the people around you are personally impacted by you.

And, while your ego might have you believe that those around you hang on your every word, spend countless hours in prayerful gratitude for you, and dedicate each day of their lives to honor you … we all know better.

Conversely, it is just as easy to step to the other end of that spectrum and draw an equally skewed perspective that completely minimizes the extent to which we personally impact those around us.

These last growing-up years with my son were filled with tasks: bedtime routines, sports activities, homework, rituals, rules, chores. But they were also filled with jokes, boyhood shenanigans, heart-to-heart talks, and some tears.

I suspect many of these tactical details will eventually slip from his memory and become embellished family lore that will be shared with the next generation over holiday tables.

What is more likely to survive the test of time is the larger sense of
purpose, connection, and vision
that those thousands of tasks ultimately created.

The greatest leaders I've known or studied all seemed to have a very clear concept of their purpose, connection, and vision. And, they structured their lives and performed daily tasks around them.

Those are the leaders who are personally impactful. *They may forget what you said, but they will never forget how you made them feel.*
Carl W. Buechner

Thanks for sharing your second cup with me.

Message 24

RITUAL

Top businesses have developed a shared culture. These places
become beloved institutions where people pour their heart and
soul into
everyday ritual and routine.
Terrence Deal

Between the years of 1964 and 1978, not a Saturday
morning went by that my brother and/or I weren't
occupied in the weekly ritual of helping our grandmother
with the task of cleaning the barroom that she owned in
the small town in which we grew up.

In an almost religious, dogmatic process, she had a very
specific methodology that guided the way in which dining
chairs were stacked, bar stools were wiped down, and
sections of floor were mopped with nothing other than
Spic and Span floor cleaner. It was a painful few hours of
work that I was sure would ultimately do me in.
As I recall, I hated every moment of every Saturday
morning I was in that bar and spent the two-and-a-half
block walk to her bar and my home in silent, expletive
seething … sure that my lot in life was unfair.

To this day, the scent of Spic and Span evokes powerful memories of the structure, discipline and unyielding inflexibility that there was to
any suggestion or hint of change to that ritual.
But looking at the ritual with some life experience and more mature eyes, I am seeing a very different side to the experience. The bar-cleaning ritual on Saturday mornings was non-negotiable. It was an absolute in my life … one that survived the test of time, economic misfortune, poor health, earnest teenage negotiations, viable out-sourcing options, and even family illness or death.
If it was Saturday morning … by God, that bar room was cleaned!
What is evident to me now, is the powerful way in which this ritual served to provide the framework around how the rest of life was managed. The structure, as constricting as it felt at times, actually provided a roadmap to help us control and manage chaos.
And, so it's logical to look at the way in which rituals impact leadership effectiveness.
A quick exercise:
Write down one or two of your own personal non-negotiable rituals that you feel define your leadership style and methodology. Be as specific as possible, e.g. your meticulous position on punctuality, or your scrupulous attention to grammar … or your unyielding position about personal dignity and respect.
Now, validate the clarity of these non-negotiables with two or three of your team members whom you trust to give you honest feedback.
If there's a disconnect, that is, your inner desires are not reflected by your external behaviors, one of them needs to be adjusted.
If there's validation, be aware of it. Recognize how

impactful it is, and understand the role it plays in making you a successful leader.

If you're having trouble with any part of this exercise, try taking a quick sniff of the floor cleaner in your household cleaner cabinet—it always does the trick for me.

Thanks for sharing your second cup with me.

Message 25

THOUGHT LEADERSHIP OR REPURPOSER?

For fans of the television show *The Office*, you've no doubt watched Michael Scott, Regional Manager at Dunder Mifflin's Scranton, PA, office in action. And you know that he's the master at taking other people's thoughts, ideas, and best practices and then incorporating them into his own leadership practices with little or no sense of context or relevance.

What Michael Scott does with unbridled hubris is called, in today's vernacular, **Repurposing**.

The concept of using other people's thoughts, ideas, or theories to further an agenda or make a point is not a new one. It's the environment in which we can readily do that and the rules of engagement for noting credit for the original thought that are in flux.

It seems that we've entered into an era where traditional plagiarism lacks the stigma of days gone by. Information, from whatever source of origin, is now spread virally through channels that seem to go at warp speed. We have 140 character sound bites that are spread

throughout the world in seconds like a 21st century game
of
"Whisper down the lane" on steroids.
Because repurposing of content has become an acceptable
way of presenting thought leadership, authority, and
credentials. It's hard to recognize who's thoughts are truly
original and who's are plucked from someone else's tweets,
blogs, or newsletters.
So, in today's culture where repurposing of content has
become an accepted practice, how can you be a thought
leader and not just a repurposer?

What follows is not repurposed. It simply represents my
own observations of how content that is not original to
the speaker can resonate with me when utilized by anyone
trying to engage me.

Here's what I want to see and feel from a speaker:
- An understanding of the core message of the repurposed
content
- Knowledge about the contextual origin of the
repurposed content
- Accurate insight into how content is currently used
- knowledge of the source credentials of the repurposed
content
- Full acknowledgement of the act of repurposing

With the above conditions met, I find myself much more
open to being engaged, giving way for the speaker to then
lead me in thought by :

- Making it **personal** to my life or job
- Making it **matter** to the situation-at-hand
- Making it **simple** to understand and apply

So, the next time you embrace a piece of re-purposed content by retweeting something, forwarding an email thread, or incorporating a quote into a presentation, answer this question:

Are you leading thought or simply repurposing someone else's thoughts?

If the answer is *both*, review the points above on how you use repurposed content in leading your life, family, team, or company.
Thanks for sharing your second cup with me.

Message 26

INTENTION

If you are a follower of Feng shui, you most likely know
about the use of a *prosperity corner* in your home or office
to manifest your intentions.
For those who have no idea of what I write, it is believed
that the far south-east corner (or gua) of your work space/
home is the area in which to
display symbols
(like the color purple, a laughing Buddha, and flowing
water)
to manifest wealth and prosperity into your
personal and professional life.
The prosperity corner display serves as a
tactile reminder of your intentions/desires
as well as a public display for all who enter your
home or work space.

It keeps you mindful of your goals and ambitions.
My limited research on Feng shui has taught me
something very interesting:

It's less about *what* you put in the gua

and more about the *intention* you assemble it with and the meaning behind the symbols you use.
In short, it's all about *conscious intention.*
Defined:
Being especially aware of a course of action one intends to follow.
Every client I work with has, at some point, reached a sought-after
milestone that is celebrated and savored.

In time, though, every milestone becomes old news, and a deeply rooted sense of restlessness to explore and move ahead can begin to emerge.
An inner voice that's saying:
"I've mastered this, now what?" … "I want different things?" …
"I'm not satisfied … it's time for a change."

This is a pivotal time when establishing a clear and conscious intention for the next step makes sense.

It's logical, but not necessarily easy … because this is also where many folks hit a wall and get stuck.
Often times, the thought of a next step can dredge up old insecurities and self-doubts. The catabolic energy surrounding change pulls you into a sense of comfort with the status quo.

Sometime, you can't quite figure out what *is* the next step you should be pursuing.
This is where the symbolic flexibility of Feng shui may help: While you may not exactly be able to articulate the next step in terms of specific positions or job titles, there

is most likely some emotional markers, or intentions, that
will help you to know when you're there:

For example: an increased sense of personal or creative
freedom, a raised level of professional **respect**, an elevated
public presence,
or an overall heightened **sense of purpose**.
Once these next step intentions are identified...
Treat them with **respect, dignity, and honor**, just as the
Feng shui follower carefully tends to the
wealth and prosperity gua in their home or office.
You might want to
surround yourself with reminders of them
(like a purple coffee mug).

Thanks for sharing your second cup with me.

Message 27

TIMING

Recently, I had the honor of being seated next to
Coach Jerry Moore, the famous head football coach of
Appalachian State University in Boone, NC, at a small
dinner party held by a friend.

Among an impressive list of accomplishments, on
September 1, 2007, Jerry Moore led Appalachian state to
score one of the biggest upsets in college football history,
defeating the then fifth-ranked Michigan Wolverines, 34-
32,
at Michigan Stadium.
Coach Moore is a humble, yet firmly convicted man
whose personal and professional accomplishments speak
for themselves. My dinner conversation with him flowed
easily on many topics ranging from motivating a team, to
instilling discipline, to fulfilling your life's purpose.
He spoke often of a book that was given to him a few
years ago that impacted him deeply. The insights he
shared with me from the book caught my interest and I

made a note to purchase the book as soon as I had the
opportunity.
The next morning, when I went online to learn more
about the book – I recognized the cover and realized that
a friend had sent me the book a few years back.

After three failed attempts to embrace the topic, engage
with the author's style, and connect with the message, I
put it on my book shelf and—in truth—forgot about it.
That day, though, I opened it up and started reading, and
as you may have guessed, I was taken in by the message
and could not put it down until I had completed the entire
book. It is now filled with notes and underlined passages.
On the inside cover, I've listed rows of page numbers of
content that particularly resonated with me.
The book is powerful … graceful in its straightforward
style and deliberate in the way the author presents his
thoughts. He emphasizes moving beyond leading a team
with the philosophy of **What's in it for them?** Rather, he
truly engages with each team member at a deeper level to
get to the heart of
What are they in it for?
Three years ago, a good friend thought the book's message
was important enough for me to read and took the time to
purchase a copy, gift wrap it, and send it to me.
But, three years ago, for whatever reason, I wasn't ready
to hear the message. Last week … I was. And, last week, I
rediscovered the book sitting on my office book shelf.
There's an old Buddhist proverb that says:
"When the student is ready, the teacher will appear."
In this case, the teacher arrived in the form of Coach Jerry
Moore. Little did I know, though, that the materials were
sent well ahead of the teacher by a caring, generous friend.

Thanks for sharing your second cup with me

PS:
The book:
The Dream Manager
by Mathew Kelly

Message 28

ACCOUNTABILITY

Accountability is the state of being answerable to someone for something within one's power, control, or management.

Whether leading a merger integration team, managing a strategic partnership, or raising spirited teenagers, we all are interdependent on accountabilities

(ours to others' and those upon which we are dependent). Personal Accountability is inherent in those promises we make to ourselves that serve as the fuel for our dreams, passions, and desires. Making commitments to ourselves is healthy, productive, and forward-thinking. In coaching, we work with clients to bring these commitments to light, to honor them, and to build strategies for bringing them to fruition.

As our lives become more complex, commitments to **self** can often become the ones that end up moving to the bottom slot on the priority list. After all, there's only so much energy and resources at our disposal. And we can easily justify prioritizing others over self with any number of cultural standards about the honorability of serving others (being selfless).

Since personal accountability is often private, it's pretty easy to dismiss it since no one else knows, and therefore, there's no fallout – or <u>so we rationalize.</u>

This is where good coaches come in to play; we don't let our clients dismiss commitments to self without some level of accountability, awareness, and evaluation of the broader consequences.

The best motivational advice I got when training for my first marathon was this:

Tell everyone you know of your intentions.

And like magic, you've expanded your sphere of accountability exponentially.

On November 13, 2010 (my 50th birthday) I made a commitment to myself to run 100 kilometers in the coming year for charities. I created a checklist, taped it to my bathroom wall and marked off each race I'd run, the number of kilometers, and the amount of money raised for the charity.

About seven months into the year, though, I'd lost steam, having completed only 38 of the 100 kilometer goal. I could not seem to reinvigorate the energy around the commitment and seriously considered taking the checklist down from my wall.

I was stuck.

So, I decided to increase the accountability stakes: For the next five months, I closed The Second Cup newsletters with a discrete fraction after my signature line that would give my subscribers an indication of my progress. (i.e. 38/100, 46/100, 71/100)

This was a subtle, but undeniable, acknowledgement of my accountability.

Each week, I found readers were noting my progress and commenting on the pace with which I was honoring my commitment. Suddenly, my goal mattered to someone other than me.

There were still times when my self-discipline lagged and I struggled to stick with it, however the public accountability I had put forth gave me the necessary incentive to keep going.
In the end, on November 12, 2011, I ran my final 10K in a record personal best time for me. And I most assuredly shared that detail in my next newsletter.

Accountability, like good coffee, is best shared. Thanks for sharing your second cup with me.

Message 29

YOUR NETWORK (CONNECTIONS & FRIENDS)

Leaders are influential in a variety of ways, not the least of which is in their **ability to influence a sphere** of colleagues, friends, family members, and associates. Social media has brought us the power of technology and global reach to replace the traditional Rolodex as a way of managing our influence potential.

How connected are you? And, what is the breadth, scope, and depth of each connection you include in your Rolodex? **How many connections do you have** in your social media platform of choice?

Here's a definition:

*Connection: [kuh-**nek**-shuh n]: something that relates or connects; a relationship or association; an acquaintance, especially one who has influence or prestige; a communications link between two points.*

As I built up my business, I invested time each day to the task of building up my portfolio of LinkeIn connections until I could boast to being in the 500+ club.

In my journey to that level, I noticed two things:

1) It became easier to adjust my definition of **connection** as I got closer to the 500 mark. The defining criteria became clouded.

2) I began to receive connection requests from folks that didn't share my definition of **connection** but seemed to want to share in being in the 500+ club.
I realized that the meaning of being in the 500+ Club is completely unique to each individual … and, my perception that it means **power, influence, success, and prestige** cannot be applied across the universe.

So, while the number may **suggest** something, I have to rely on traditional methods of assessing leadership influence that extend beyond
the new and flashy technology gadgets – instinct, **personal interaction, reputation, thought leadership**.
Knowing how many connections I have (500+), you could draw any one or more of the following conclusions:
- I've established a solid reputation and built a sound network of professional contacts that I can count on to clear calendar time to help me out if/when I reach out to them.
- My sphere of influence is significant in size, scope, and diversity.
- I know a lot of people.
- A lot of people know me .
Of course, I realize you could also draw one of these conclusions:
- I'll connect with anyone who can stroke the keys of a computer and request to connect.
- As long as our last names share at least one vowel and one consonant in common, I'll connect with you.

- If I read your name tag on a trade show floor … we're connected.
What is your criteria for 'connecting'?
Which of the above align with your strategy ?

Thanks for sharing your second cup with me.

Message 30

FEAR

Ever think like this? "I know that something has to change.
but, the devil I know ... "

Most times, we are aware that we need to change,
but we are blocked by fear. What kind of fear?

It's the fear that if we give up what we have, what we do,
or what we know, the alternative could be worse, or more
difficult, or potentially harmful. And so, we decide that
the "devil" we know might not be so bad to live with until
we have something known, proven, and low-risk to replace
it with.

This can often result in longterm inertia as we grow more
and more fearful of that "devil" we haven't met yet.
One way to break that cycle is to allow yourself to just
simply cease the existing behavior you want to change

and give yourself some breathing room. Don't think about replacing or filling in the space just yet, relax and enjoy the task of just **making space**.

It's like that cathartic feeling of cleaning out the basement, garage, or attic.

Pema Chodron, in her book *The Places that Scare You: A Guide to Fearlessness in Difficult Times*, refers to this place as the "in between state where the warrior spends a lot of time growing up." It is the place that she says, 'by not knowing, not hoping to know, and not acting like we know what's happening,
we access our inner strength."
It's a place where our skills are called into action, our resolve is put to the test, and our faith becomes more than a theory.
Next time you find yourself even thinking "The devil I know,"
try one of these endings:

1. **Could be 10 times worse than the devil I haven't met yet ...**

2. **Is choking the life out of me ....**

.

3. **Has tricked me into thinking this is the best it will ever be ...**

Give them a try … they just might make the "in between" spaces
less intimidating and give you a push in the direction you want to go.

Thanks for sharing your second cup with me.

Message 31

ACCEPTANCE

In times like these, it helps to recall that there have always been times like these.

- Paul Harvey

It's easy to get swept up into negative group-think:

"This is the worst economic crisis EVER - there are no opportunities, only despair."

"My age is my biggest liability in today's job market."

"There is no record anywhere of a more difficult, demanding, and unreasonable client."

"It's all China's fault."

"Technology has made me obsolete."

Instead of placing a label on the situation you are facing that feeds into the above catabolic energy, try cutting your sentence short like this:

Mike Malinchok

The current economy simply **is**.
The client I'm working with simply **is.**
My age simply **is**.
The new technology simply **is**.

Now flip your energy toward identifying and articulating
why, how, where and when do
you **uniquely** bring value to what **is**.

This will shift the power back to **you**
and away from fueling the
energy that hungrily wants to change or control what **is**.

Here's a thought:
In just a few years, it's a pretty safe bet that some of us
will be looking back on these times as the "good old days"
when we were young.

Thanks for sharing your second cup with me.

An extra 'shot' for your second cup:

I have decided to approach this year's goal setting exercise
in a way that establishes consistent <u>daily</u> accountability
and allows me to have flexibility in my actions to adjust to
new paths that
will inevitably arise
throughout the year.
My intention is to create daily rituals that will engage me
at the start and end of each day where accountability will
be more focused on RIGHT NOW versus a
distant, end-of-year target.

After much introspection and honest assessment of needs,
I've created and embraced the daily mantra of :
'P.N.C.'

Here's what it stands for:

PURGE
*Purge your world of the things that are limiting you, whether
it's the clutter in your basement, garage, and closets..........OR
the personal beliefs, professional perspectives, and world views
that are past their prime.*

NOURISH
*Nourish your body to deliver the kind of performance you
need to fulfill your life's purpose. Eat clean, whole, and
consistently throughout the day. Supplement with nutrients
you know are recommended based on your own personal
health needs.*

CHALLENGE

Challenge yourself to consistently go one step further than what is expected in at least one daily activity. For example, jog just 5 more minutes after that 3 mile run ....or, <u>give your client just one more deliverable of value from you than what he or she is expecting</u>.....or, give your loved one just one more hug as they head out for the day.

If you're stumped on this last one (Challenge), try inserting this question at the end of your interactions with family, clients, or colleagues:

"What else can I do to help you today?"

Of the three PNC components above, I know that PURGING is the one that will most likely be my greatest hurdle each day to knock down.

A curious thing happened as I was about to 'save' and 'publish' this edition of The Second Cup - I received the following message in my in-box (from a daily e-source for inspiration that I subscribe to):

"Empty yourself and let the universe fill you"

Thanks for sharing your Second Cup with me and ,today, think PURGE, NOURISH, CHALLENGE - PNC!

Images by

Jennifer S. Beavers
'I've always loved the beauty of nature and often I'm told
I have an "eye" for photography. It's my belief that we all
have an eye for the world. The images I capture are my
unique view and expression of it.
As I grow as a photographic artist, I'm experiencing nature
in a more intimate way through my camera. It continues
to be a life enriching experience. I see more. Celebrate
more. Savor more. Remember more. Enjoy more.
Appreciate more.
My sincerest hope is my work will allow others to savor
the beauty in the world — especially the details found in
nature.'
Contact: Jennifer@jenniferbeavers.com

Edited by

Don Munro
Owner, Writing that Sells
Business writer, editor, communications consultant and
media relations specialist assists companies of all sizes
publicize products, services and news.
Contact: munrodh@optonline.net

Made in the USA
Middletown, DE
05 January 2023